THE GREAT RESET: CHARTING

THE WAY FORWARD

THE GREAT RESET: CHARTING

THE WAY FORWARD

David P B Orton

LOGOS IMPRINT
Lifemessenger Inc.
Melbourne, Australia

Lifemessenger Inc.
PO Box 777, Mount Eliza, Victoria
Australia

ISBN 978-0-6450989-0-7

Preface

These two articles were written, one for Advent 2020 and the other early 2021, with the thought of the *World Economic Forum* (WEF) meeting in Davos, Switzerland in January 2021 under the banner, *The Great Reset*.

This conference represents the world's most powerful elites – politicians, royalty, government bureaucrats, academics, economists, conservationists, public health experts, Big Money, Big Tech, Big Pharma, Big Media, and Hollywood celebrities – seeking to recreate the world in their own image.

With the West's rejection of her Christian past she has also denounced the cultural and social substructures that have provided her freedom and prosperity. From the Enlightenment onwards, for some 300 years, she has pursued other gods. As we negotiate this first half of the 21st century, the full harvest of her apostasy from the personal, infinite God is coming to maturity. We have sown a wind and are reaping a whirlwind (Hos 8:7).

Nevertheless, God's judgments are redemptive. Regardless of Western man's rebellion, he still lives in God's world. No matter how much he pursues his utopian dreams – attempting to recover Eden without God – recreating the world through his own fiat word, he comes up against the world as it really is. All facts stubbornly remain God-created facts. There is no escape. God's image in man and creative imprint in the world are inerasable.

Through God's providence and predetermined plan, the West will ultimately awake from her delusion. Reaping the consequences of her rebellion – economically, societally, and psychologically – she will come to what Cornelius Van Til calls "epistemological self-consciousness"—to the realization of the incoherence of her belief-system and that it bears no relation to reality. Autonomous-man's intellectual precommitments when extrapolated do not comport with the way the world is. His precommitments and his fiat decrees of anticipated utopia instead lead to the abyss. God's judgments enforce reality.

But for this "epistemological self-consciousness" to occur, the church, as the pillar and ground of truth, must first come to hers. That the same precommitments, even for the church, lead to the same abyss. Forsaking modernism and subjectivism she must return to the verities of "the faith once for all delivered to the saints", to historic biblical orthodoxy. To the absolute and inerrant God whose word is clear, sufficient, and unchangeable—providing the wisdom and laws for man's prosperity in God's world.

The good news is that Christ's resurrection and ascension have secured the beachhead in the enemy's territory. And now through his church the invasion has begun. Despite momentary setbacks no satanic authority can, nor will, withstand the advance of God's Kingdom in the world. Christ's rule and law-word will prevail in history, outworking in a new worldwide Christian civilization. To this end this booklet is dedicated.

D. P. B. Orton
Cape Schanck, Victoria
Australia Day, 26th January 2021

THE GREAT RESET:

CHARTING THE WAY FORWARD

In 2004 I wrote that the period 1950 to 2025 represents a hinge of history, on which swings a door to a new epoch of the Kingdom of God. The Biden presidency will bring us to the brink of that new era, to 2025.

But at the same time I also wrote that the "twin towers" attack of 2001 signalled an acceleration of God's judgment on the West, already reaching through the holocaust of two world-wars. Parallel to the rise of the Islamic Jihad, however, has been that of militant secular-humanism hand-in-glove with cultural-Marxism, and their usurpation of the West's institutions—of its legislatures, courts, universities, media, and corporate boardrooms.

The Biden presidency, in tandem with the global elites and the COVID-19 pandemic's convenient segue into the *World Economic Forum's* (WEF) "Great Reset" of 2021, will bring these movements to full maturity. All designed, through dislocation of civil society and economic lock-down, to lead the world's compliant masses into a dystopian nightmare of global governance where all personal property is willingly surrendered for a universal basic income. This objective and more is outlined in the WEF's published documents. If this were not so, their plans are so bizarre it would not be believable.

The lead-time of God's mercy has expired. So, how must the church respond to this? And how will she navigate the new cultural and political terrain?

There are five things that she must reject and five that she must retain:

1. Partisan politics for *the politics of the Kingdom,*
2. The myth of neutrality for *a cultural gospel,*
3. Experientialism and false prophecy for *the Scriptures,*
4. Tribalism and sectarianism for *apostolic unity,* and
5. Eschatologies of defeat for *Christ's victory in history.*

Partisan politics for *the politics of the Kingdom*

First, she must reject *partisan politics* for the politics of the Kingdom of God. She must rediscover that the law-word of God provides the blueprint not only for personal salvation but also cultural redemption. Every political party and ideology must, therefore, be called up to the benchmark of God's word.

This is not to ignore the fact that not all political parties are equal. Some more closely represent Christian verities than others. While the left (progressivism and socialism) is inherently statist, the right (individual freedom/responsibility and free-enterprise) historically championed limited government. However, while the conservative wing of politics inherited its values from the Judeo-Christian tradition, of individual freedom and responsibility, with the West's rejection of its Christian foundations there is increasingly less distinction of right from left. The former infiltrated by the latter's cultural-Marxism, blurring policy distinctions, both social and fiscal.

As a manifestation of autonomous-man, they alike pursue *salvation through politics*. They seek to recover Paradise by coercion from the top down. For example, the WEF's "Global Reset", true to its humanistic urge to Paradise, advocates stronger state control and global governance to arrest "fragmentation" and "entropy", of which, in their view, nationalism is the primary symptom. Evidenced in recent years, for example, by Brexit and the election of Trump. This is assuming of course the Marxist interventionist economics, as the WEF does, and the state's warrant to redistribute wealth. They merely project onto the global economy this ideology's need for centralized control.

Nonetheless, the politics of *nationalism* (e.g., Trumpism) and *globalism* (e.g., EU, Democrats, GOP) both similarly appeal to increased centralized power and thence to force. Culturally, on the extreme end of the spectrum, this appeal to force is illustrated in the recent storming of the Capitol in Washington DC by ultra-right-wing protesters; or alternatively, on the other end of the spectrum, the wide-spread riots after Trump's election and Big Tech's kneejerk censorship of conservative politicians President Trump and retired US congressman Ron Paul subsequent to the Capitol attack, including the de-platforming of *Parler* as a venue for alternative views. This alliance of Big Tech with the left haply coincides with the WEF's advocacy of the surveillance-state, especially accelerated by COVID-19 tracing. Conservatives, from centre-right to far-right, along with the left, all resort to increased authoritarian control of society, whether through the state or other agencies. This is seen in the increased state control of monetary policy (i.e., over central banks) so as to ensure sufficient government funding to meet the challenge of COVID-19 and to artificially shore-up economies after the shock of the lock-downs. This increased money supply will only exacerbate the boom-bust cycle of inflation-deflation and accelerate an eventual depression. All sourced in the immorality of counterfeit money created by fractional reserve banking.

Engendered by COVID-19 panic, an abnormally compliant populace is being conditioned. Draconian "lock-downs" (significantly, prison terminology), mask-wearing, social-distancing, work from home, loss of employment and income, increased reliance on government handouts, over-policing, and disproportionate penalties for non-compliance, are all tearing at the fabric of a free civil society, producing isolation from and distrust of fellow-citizens, and above all submission to the state's rule by decree.

This coercion and compliance of the populace has also occurred through the gazetting of so-called "hate crimes". In the name of "antidiscrimination" and "justice" the legislature and the executive encroach upon the West's historic liberties: freedom of association, freedom of expression, and especially freedom of religion. Whether from the far left (communist) or the far right (fascist), *salvation by politics* is inevitably totalitarian: for example, the fascist dictatorship of Nazi Germany including its suppression of communism; and Franco's nationalist suppression of the same during the Spanish civil war; or, alternatively, the communist one party systems of the Soviet Union and Communist China and their totalitarian denial of human rights, and Robespierre's tyranny during the French revolution. In each case anarchy – moral, societal, and political – led to tyranny.

Similar to these historical examples of *both* fascist and communistic regimes, the West's cultural and political tumult is arcing toward totalitarianism as it disingenuously employs the language of "freedom" and "fairness" – dancing to the tune of political correctness – for legislative change and authoritarian gain. All hues of the political spectrum, in differing measures, resort to this revolutionist copy-book propaganda and disinformation, subverting the meaning of language and thereby truth. Hence also the present phenomenon of "fake news", belying the media's supposed objectivity and exposing its complicity in the West's cultural revolution. History demonstrates that revolutions must commandeer both the courts and the media to suppress the masses.

So what is the answer? To rebuild a free and open society demands that the Christian church recover a *political theory grounded in the Sovereignty of God.* And this can only be discovered in the triune God of the Bible, in whom the age-old conflict of "the one and the many" is resolved.

Political theory and history oscillates between these two polarities: from the "the one" (tyranny) to the "the many" (anarchy) and back again. The one inevitably leads to the other. Only under the sovereign God – who is himself a tri-unity of Father, Son, and Spirit (the three-in-one) – can each sphere of society be sovereign and yet not violate another. The Godhead is thus the ground and paradigm for man's social relationships; all individuals and societal spheres are *ontologically equal* but *economically different.* From the individual, to the family, the church, to civil society and the state; while all equal under God, each functions within its distinct sphere. None presides governmentally over another beyond its biblically defined role. Nonetheless, they do overlap and interrelate according to each function. For example, the state does have jurisdiction over an individual, family, or even a church, if a legitimate criminal law – that is, a biblically warranted one – is broken. Building on John Calvin, Abraham Kuyper, theologian, prime minister of the Netherlands, and founder of the Free University of Amsterdam, was the pioneer of this notion of sphere sovereignty.

Under the doctrine of *sphere sovereignty*, as developed further by American Episcopalian scholar, Ray Sutton, the Kingdom of God comes progressively through four covenantal spheres: *individual > family > church > state*. And this occurs according to a progressive principle of *internal integrity* leading to *external integration*. Beginning with the individual, *internal integrity* (i.e., inner health according to each sphere's biblically defined nature and function) enables each sphere to *integrate externally* with the next sphere. Healthy individuals integrate with the next largest sphere, the family; healthy families integrate with the next, the church; and healthy churches integrate with civil society and the state. This ensures, beginning in the regeneration of the individual, that all spheres of society are renewed by the Kingdom of God, not through coercion, but through the power of the Gospel from the bottom up. All other spheres of society arc from one or more of these covenantal spheres; for example: education not only arcs from the family but also the church (not the state!); and economics arcs from the individual, family, and church (but not the state!). In fact, the state has no biblical warrant to engage in monetary policy or banking, let alone creating fiat currency through fractional reserve banking. The free market working under biblical law would solve our monetary problems.

In the politics of the Kingdom, government is pluralistic. Beginning in self-government it is shared by all spheres, each according to their biblical role. The state is not supreme; its authority is warranted and delimited by God's word, and it governs only by consent of the individual. And hence, the humanistic drift to *statism* is forestalled. Even so, it must be noted that the state's authority, as biblically defined (Rom 13:1-7), is coercive; it is the institution of compulsion. And as such will inevitably operate accordingly if it transgresses beyond its delimited role into the other spheres. Hence, the dangerous potential of the state.

Sphere sovereignty, however, does not preclude, but rather mandates Christian involvement in the political sphere, although not through an aberrant urge to Paradise, through coercive power. Rather, the Gospel of the Kingdom of God is the power of God to salvation and to Paradise. It is only the atoning death and resurrection of Christ that reverses sin and its results— "fragmentation" and "entropy". Since Christ's resurrection the world is no longer running down. Despite sin, because God is both Creator and Redeemer, the cosmos – as man's habitation – is not only sufficient and secure but also under renovation. God not only sustains what he creates but also redeems it.

The doctrines of *creation* and *salvation* form a coherent whole. Through the resurrection of Christ and the preaching of the Gospel the time-space world (the *created* world) *has* entered the regeneration and *is now* being rehabilitated. We are living in the administration of the fulness of times when God is bringing *all things* into one head, Christ (Eph 1:10; also Col 1:13-23). *All* spheres of society, including the state, are integral to God's Kingdom on earth.

The Gospel is thus the saving agency, not the state, nor for that matter, the church. *Partisan* politics and the state are, therefore, not the Kingdom of God. Nonetheless, to the degree politics and the state yield to the *absolute* and *ultimate* authority of God and his law-word, they can serve it. The Bible contains blueprints for the role of the state (e.g., justice), for health (e.g., quarantine laws), banking and finance (e.g., prohibition of multiple indebtedness of a single asset, i.e., a prohibition of fractional reserve banking), and so on. If *biblical* law was implemented COVID-19 would be halted and our economic problems solved, and with our individual freedoms intact (e.g., biblical quarantine law does not quarantine the healthy!).

Subsequently, Christian involvement in politics is expressed in two ways: *first*, as citizens, by fulfilling their duty to vote or, additionally, by a vocational call to politics; and *second*, corporately through the church's priestly duty to pray for all in authority and to teach the state her role under God and his word (*cf.* 1 Tim 2:1-4; Mt 28:18-20; Rom 13:1-7). But in both cases, the state is viewed as a *delegated* authority under the triune God of the Bible, not as an *autonomous* authority. Christ is Lord not Caesar.

Precisely because "the Kingdom of God is not *of* this world" (Jn 18:36), we need not resort to political saviours and quick-fixes—to partisan politics and power. If we do, it is because, like the world, we see the state as having more power than God in the here and now. Furthermore, like the world, we are merely preserving our own "personal peace and affluence", not bringing the Kingdom of God.

God's servants therefore appeal to a higher power, which is the very point of John 18:36. As a worldling Pilate presumed the authority of his political office over Jesus, provoking Jesus' response, "You would have no authority over me at all unless it had been given you *from* above" (Jn 19:11). As Paul also taught concerning the institution of the state, "there is no authority except *from* God" (Rom 13:1).

Consequently, God's authority extends to the state as instituted by him and is therefore accountable to him. For this very reason the church's teaching ministry also extends to the state. As his servant it is obligated to obey and uphold his righteous laws (Rom 13:1-7). This therefore also mandates Christian resistance within certain bounds. When the state transgresses its divinely instituted limits the Christian must obey God rather than men (Acts 5:29).

The problem, however, of partisan politics cannot be solved without first exploding the myth of neutrality.

The myth of neutrality for *a cultural gospel*

Second, she must reject the *myth of neutrality* for a cultural gospel. This demands an entire world-and-life-view grounded in the sovereignty of God. Without it we are not able to develop the politics of the Kingdom of God. God's sovereignty, as both Creator and Redeemer, over the totality of human existence necessarily includes politics. Created, male and female, in the image of God, man is therefore a covenant creature. Every person is thus a covenant-keeper or covenant-breaker, and is inherently religious, either worshiping the creator-God or the creature (Rom 1:18-32). Man is not neutral: neither religiously, ethically, nor intellectually. Apart from grace he is at enmity with God.

Secularism, therefore, is not a benign ideology. The notion that the secular-state is neutral must be seen for what it is—a delusion of the first water. Jesus said, "Whoever is not with me is against me" (Lk 11:23).

What applies for individuals applies also for their corporate life in the state. There is no neutrality. Whether as an individual or in his corporate expression through the state, man either worships the true God or a false god. As Henry Van Til rightly observed, "Culture is religion externalized".

With the Enlightenment and our present hyper-modernism, man is now his own ultimate reference point, his own god, determining his own reality. And this plays out in the state. Every state inevitably legislates *somebody's* law. It will either be the sovereign creator-God's or autonomous-man's. There is no middle ground. No system of law is religiously or morally neutral.

It has been rightly said that when a nation changes its god, it changes its laws. The West's cultural amnesia, wilfully forgetting her Christian foundations and forsaking the personal infinite-God, has led the English speaking West to a shift from common law to positivist law. The former entails the humility of *interpretation* (Biblical precedent law), whereas the latter entails the hubris of *creation* (Roman legislative law). With the rejection of its origins the West has turned its back on *transcendent law* for purely *immanent law*, and thus the tyranny of man's law over man. As a result there is no appeal beyond man-made law—"the law of the Medes and the Persians". Law, as the random product of a materialistic closed-system, is thus considered as a "social construct", as evolving and mutable, responding to changing times and conditions. It is thus shaped by the vagaries of passing fads and fashions. As a result, in a relativistic world one man's food is another man's poison; what is freedom to one is slavery to another. Thus the overturning of the age-old

Christian definitions of marriage, family, sexuality, and human significance. With the rejection of the world-and-life-view of man – male and female – made in the image of God, human life as inherently sacred has been lost. This has opened the door to legalized abortion, euthanasia, and assisted suicide. Instead of protecting life the West has become a culture of death.

The Christian church must therefore rediscover *the law of God in antithesis to the law of autonomous-man.* As concomitant, it must also rediscover that it is not antithetical to the gospel; that, in fact, the Law *and* the Gospel are the foundation of not only of Christianity but also of justice and law for society. And allied to this is the recovery of the biblical doctrine of the state as under God (Rom 13:1-7), and its corollary, the rejection of secularism's *myth of neutrality*. This then demands a Christian state. Not an *ecclesiocracy* (rule by clerics), but rather a *theocracy* (rule by God). While this may affirm the separation of spheres, of church and state, it does not affirm the separation of Christianity - of God – from the civil state. Contrary to popular mythology the First Amendment of the American constitution makes no reference to the separation of church and state; rather it simply states that "Congress shall make no law respecting an establishment of religion, or prohibiting the free exercise thereof... .". The founders' concern was not to institute *a particular denomination* as an established church over another (Jefferson). Furthermore there is no evidence in the Constitution, the acts of Congress, or in the constitutions or the laws of the various states that stipulate a separation of church and state. Rather, the opposite is the case; a number of the states had established churches after the First

Amendment and their constitutions were not religiously neutral (e.g., Connecticut, Delaware, Maryland, Massachusetts, North Carolina).

Only a state that places ultimacy in the triune God can offer true freedom. The alternative is a state that places ultimacy in man—in human tyranny. Even a democracy is a dictatorship of the 51% majority. Only a state under the God of the Bible can provide individual freedom, although held in balanced tension with individual responsibility. From its first-century origins, by refusing Caesar as lord, Christianity injected into world history the notion of *limited* government, the pagan world being dominated by absolute state power, beyond which there was no appeal.

Only the Gospel of the Kingdom of God – of God's government on earth – offers individual and political freedom.

Experientialism and false prophecy for *the Scriptures*

Third, she must reject *experientialism and false prophecy* for the Scriptures. This is not to deny the subjective experience of the *living* God, the biblical exercise of the charismata, or the ministry of the prophet. But it is to discern between this and *absolutizing* subjective experience above him and, thus, false dependence on prophets and prophecy. And this must also include absolutizing experiential phenomena, whether genuine manifestations of the Spirit or not. These are particularly the sins of the charismatic stream of the church. Having refused a corrective word during the 1960s-80s through what became known as the

Shepherding movement (Derek Prince, Bob Mumford, Ern Baxter, Charles Simpson et al.), in broad brushstrokes, the renewal has now gone to seed and been trodden underfoot of men—by imposters and the immature who prophesy from their *own* spirit.

And so, "Thus says the Lord GOD, Woe to the foolish prophets who follow their own spirit, and have seen nothing!" (Ezek 13:3). This has been dramatically exposed in the recent US election and demands accountability and repentance. Tellingly, Pat Robertson, founder of CBN, who was instrumental in the rejection of the corrective word through Bob Mumford and Ern Baxter in the 1970s-80s, has been one of the more strident voices "prophesying" a Trump second-term victory. Too many out of their own spirits have falsely prophesied an outcome that has not transpired. Whether the electoral outcome is fraudulent or not, for the moment, is beside the point.

Peter's words must be heeded:

> 19 And we have the prophetic word more fully confirmed, to which you will do well to pay attention as to a lamp shining in a dark place, until the day dawns and the morning star rises in your hearts, 20 knowing this first of all, that no prophecy of Scripture comes from someone's own interpretation. 21 For no prophecy was ever produced by the will of man, but men spoke from God as they were carried along by the Holy Spirit.

2 Peter 1:19–21

These words of Peter are bookended by his own supernatural experience as an eyewitness of the majesty and the problem of false prophets and teachers. What Peter claims here is momentous. He is saying that the prophetic word of Scripture is even more sure than his own experience of the Lord at the Mount of Transfiguration. The ministry and life of the incarnate Son of God, as sure as that is, is made even *more sure* by the Scriptures. This is a weighty claim that must be taken to heart by the renewal stream. Our subjective experience of God must yield to the authority of Scripture—to sound theology and doctrine.

In a time of judgment upon God's people Isaiah commands them not to fear "conspiracy" but rather to fear the LORD. They are to return from the occult prognosticators to "the law and the testimony":

> 11 For the LORD spoke thus to me with a strong hand, and instructed me that I should not walk in the way of this people, saying:
>
> 12 "Do not say, 'A conspiracy,'
>
> Concerning all that this people call a conspiracy,
>
> Nor be afraid of their threats, nor be troubled.
>
> 13 The LORD of hosts, Him you shall hallow;
>
> Let Him be your fear,
>
> And let Him be your dread.
>
> 14 He will be as a sanctuary,
>
> But a stone of stumbling and a rock of offense
>
> To both the houses of Israel,
>
> As a trap and a snare to the inhabitants of Jerusalem.
>
> 15 And many among them shall stumble;
>
> They shall fall and be broken,
>
> Be snared and taken."

16 Bind up the testimony,

Seal the law among my disciples.

17 And I will wait on the LORD,

Who hides His face from the house of Jacob;

And I will hope in Him.

18 Here am I and the children whom the LORD has given me!

We are for signs and wonders in Israel

From the LORD of hosts,

Who dwells in Mount Zion.

19 And when they say to you, "Seek those who are mediums and wizards, who whisper and mutter," should not a people seek their God? Should they seek the dead on behalf of the living? 20 To the law and to the testimony! If they do not speak according to this word, it is because there is no light in them.

Isaiah 8:11–20 NKJV

What some call conspiracy, God calls judgment. So, in the face of the Assyrian onslaught the battle-cry of God's people ought to be—"To the law and to the testimony!" Not—"To the soothsayers and diviners!"

Rather, they are to "Bind up the testimony" and "Seal the law among his disciples." God's Law is the touchstone of the prophetic. Every true prophet of God will call the people of God back to the law of the covenant. This is why Paul, in a prophetic spirit, declares that "*All* Scripture is breathed out by God and profitable for teaching, for reproof, for correction, and for training in righteousness" (2 Tim 3:16). This means that the *entire* corpus of Scripture, especially the laws and ordinances of the OT, are for us today. Not as a means of justification, as the Judaizers, but rather sanctification—as a charter for life (Lev 18:5). Not only for the individual Christian but also for society. This is the Reformer's traditional "second use of the law". And it must logically include the judicial and civil law as the application of the Ten Commandments, which are merely the summary statement of the *entire* Law.

Like Moses, Jesus also provides a summary statement. When asked as to the greatest commandment he renews the Law by rehearsing the *shema* of Deuteronomy 6:

> 29 Jesus answered, "The most important is, 'Hear, O Israel: The Lord our God, the Lord is one. 30 And you shall love the Lord your God with all your heart and with all your soul and with all your mind and with all your strength.' 31 The second is this: 'You shall love your neighbor as yourself.' There is no other commandment greater than these."

Mark 12:29–31

The entire Law of God is encompassed in this renewal. And so, the NT people of God, as "a royal priesthood and holy nation" (1 Pet 2:9), can now make known the manifold wisdom of God to the rulers and authorities in the heavenly places (Eph 3:10):

> 5 See, I have taught you statutes and rules, as the LORD my God commanded me, that you should do them in the land that you are entering to take possession of it. 6 Keep them and do them, for that will be your wisdom and your understanding

in the sight of the peoples, who, when they hear
all these statutes, will say, 'Surely this great
nation is a wise and understanding people.'

Deuteronomy 4:5–6

The charismatic church must, therefore,
without forsaking the exercise of the charismata, repent
of its unbiblical reliance on prophets and prophecy
(whether false or otherwise) and return to biblical
expository preaching, and to *sola scriptura*. Not to
mention the personality cults, the idolatry of
phenomenon, and monetizing of the gospel, that is so
dominant in that stream. Furthermore, she must teach
and apply the biblical disciplines for the exercise of the
charismata as taught by Paul. This *must* include the
excommunication of false prophets and teachers when
necessary (Ex 22:18; Lev 19:26, 31; 20:27; Dt 13:1-5;
17:7, 12; 18:10-14, 20-22; Jer. 2:8; 14:14, 15; Zech.
13:3; 1 Cor 5:9-13; 12:10; 14:29; 1 Tim 1:3-7; 4:11;
5:20; 6:2-10, 20; 2 Tim 2:16; 3:1-9; 4:1-5, 14; Tit 1:9-
14; 2:15; 2 Pet 2; 1 Jn 4:1).

As a result, both the renewal and Reformed
streams must do business with not only the true ministry
of the Holy Spirit but also that of true apostles and
prophets, in particular.

For the Reformed this will mean honouring
sola scriptura above human reason. Cessationism rejects
the plain meaning of the text by imposing an extra-
biblical, semi-dispensational frame over God's word,
arguing that the gifts and ministries of the Spirit were
exclusively for the apostolic era so as to confirm the
canon. The gifts and ministries of the Spirit are *not* for us
today! However, this flies in the face of Scripture; it is

embarrassingly devoid of any such statement, explicit or implicit. To the contrary, what *is* explicit is that the *gift of prophecy*, for example, is not for the confirmation of the canon but rather for the church's "edification and exhortation and comfort" (1 Cor 14:3 NKJV). The cessationist must therefore claim that the church no longer has this need. Really? It is also falsified by the fact that not all first-century apostles were canonical, also falsifying the cessation of the apostolic ministry, which I will address momentarily. Although this is not to deny the unique Scripture-writing role of some first-century apostles. Furthermore the cessationist accusation that prophecy, subsequent to the canon, implies an illicit continuity of equal authority from the OT and apostolic eras into the entire NT era denies not only the continuity of the covenant but also progressive revelation. Hebrews underscores the seriousness of rejecting a greater covenant with greater promises (Heb 8:6):

> 2 For since the message declared by angels proved to be reliable, and every transgression or disobedience received a just retribution, 3 how shall we escape if we neglect such a great salvation? It was declared at first by the Lord, and it was attested to us by those who heard, 4 while God also bore witness by signs and wonders and various miracles and by gifts of the Holy Spirit distributed according to his will.
>
> Hebrews 2:2–4

Moving from the OT to the NT, rather than a decrease of revelation, authority and power, there is an increase because revelation is progressive. And so, when the apostles went forth preaching, the Lord worked with them, confirming the word with signs following (Mk 16:20). Although, the reason we don't see this more today is because of the rationalism and unbelief of the Western church and culture; even Jesus was hindered from doing many mighty works, because of unbelief (Mt 15:38). Nonetheless, in the NT there is an increase for God's prophets, although accompanied by a concomitant accountability. The gifts and operations of the Spirit are given precisely to underscore not only the increase of revelation and glory under a greater covenant but also the increase of judgment. There is a higher standard for the NT prophet—greater light, greater judgment. This greater judgment is reflected in the Pauline directive to "judge" prophecy, i.e., to weigh or evaluate it (1 Cor 14:29; 1 Thes 5:20-21).

Nevertheless, compared to the canonical prophets and the archetypal prophets, Moses and Elijah, the NT prophet is not on the same level. Yet there is a clear continuity of the function from OT to NT of the prophet as God's covenant-enforcer (e.g., the apostle-prophet John [see Rev 2:5; 22:9]); the prophet is God's attorney, prosecuting his covenant-lawsuit not only against his people but also against kings and nations. While the prophet may exercise a *gift of prophecy*, *words of knowledge* or *words of wisdom* (1 Cor 12:4-11), the burden of the prophet is to call God's people back to covenant fidelity, to his law-word. They are thus not prognosticators or soothsayers. It is crucial to note here the distinction between two levels of the prophetic: the *gift of prophecy* (1 Cor 12) and the *ministry of the prophet* (Eph 4). They are vastly different in grace and authority; the former is purely for "edification and exhortation and comfort" (1 Cor 14:3 NKJV), while the latter is a word-ministry that includes correction and rebuke (2 Tim 3:16).

So, rather than merely equal authority with the OT prophet, with the increase of revelation and glory, the NT prophet speaks with a greater authority—as God's representative they too declare, "Thus says the LORD". This assumes, of course, they remain true to the law and the testimony as mentioned above. Additionally, the cessationist claim upon 1 Corinthians 13:10 – "but when the perfect comes, the partial will pass away" – is exegetically untenable. Rather than the *canon*, the "perfect" (*telos*) refers to the *consummation* (see Calvin). Rather than a cessationist text, this is a continuationist one! Paul states the precise opposite to cessationism; that the gifts continue from the first-century through to the consummation. Then, Paul says, we shall see the Lord "face to face", no longer knowing partially but fully (13:12). In other words, at *that* point gifts will cease because they are no longer needed. Nor can the day of Pentecost be claimed exclusively as a once-for-all event. The outpouring of the Spirit on the day of Pentecost not only signals redemption *accomplished* – once-for-all – but also redemption *applied*—it is thus not only the *inauguration* of Christ's Kingdom but also its *continuation* through to *consummation* at the second advent. From Pentecost onward, the gifts and ministries of the Spirit are, therefore, integral to the Kingdom of God's progress in history (Mt 12:28; Mk 9:1; Jn 3:5; Acts 2:17-18; Rom 14:17; 15:19; 1 Cor 2:4; 4:20; 6:11; 12:4, 7, 8, 9, 11, 13; 15:24ff).

The Kingdom is hence a dispensation of the Spirit, as Paul underlines to the Romans: "The kingdom of

God…is *in the Holy Spirit*" (14:17). Minimal Holy Spirit, minimal Kingdom progress—a lesson here one would think. Any argument that leads us to brazenly reject the Word of God which commands us negatively, "*Do not* quench the Spirit. *Do not* despise prophecies" (1 Thes 5:19–20) and positively, "Pursue love, and *earnestly desire* the spiritual gifts, especially that you may prophesy" (1 Cor 14:1), should strike us with the fear of God. The strict cessationist position is one of unbelief and rebellion against God. One thing that has not *ceased*—our need for repentance, a radical change of mind. For the sake of the Kingdom of God it is time for the Reformed world to repent of the limitations they have placed on the omnipotent Spirit of God.

For the renewal it will mean honouring *sola scriptura* above prophetic revelation. I have already dealt with this above.

Both streams fall foul of a crucial hermeneutical principle: *holding truth in balanced tension*. This comes into play in the handling of seeming opposites, of paradoxes in Scripture. We violate this principle to our own peril—for then we fall into *errors of emphasis*, as distinct from doctrinal-creedal errors. The Reformed by rejecting the plain meaning of the text fall foul of a rationalistic position, ironically leading to irrationalistic arguments to explain away the text. It makes nonsense of the word of God, and is hence anti-*sola scriptura*. Men's arguments trump the word of God and deny his power. If, however, the word of God is accepted at face value, we can then work out what ceases and what continues. This means that cessationism and continuationism are not antithetical but rather a continuum or spectrum. Regardless of one's present position, whether accurate or not, it will be a mix of both. For example the strict cessationist does not deny the continuing role of the Holy Spirit in guidance, whether personal or corporate, or that John Knox was popularly considered the *apostle* to Scotland, and so on; or the strict continuationist will not deny that canonical writing has ceased. However "a *false balance* is an abomination to the Lord" (Prov 11:1; 20:23). It is imperative therefore to find the *true balance*, in light of Scripture, in this regard. There *is* a biblically balanced location on the continuum. Put very simply, the canon has ceased, the ministry of the Spirit continues. Once this is settled *biblically*, we can still err in emphasis *practically* one way or the other at any point in time. We must learn in our experience the balanced tension between Word and Spirit—it has been well said: *All Word, you dry up; all Spirit, you blow up!*

In closing a comment must be made concerning the foundational ministries of *apostles and prophets* (Eph 2:20; 4:11; 1 Cor 12:28). Again using the reformational principle of the plain meaning of the text and *sola scriptura*, thus prohibiting any arbitrary dispensational framework imposed over the text, these ministries have clearly continued throughout the history of the Christian movement, though not always explicitly recognised at the time. Nonetheless, the biblical function of each can be traced within history.

The five ascension-gift ministries of Ephesians 4:11 – apostles, prophets, evangelists, shepherds, and teachers – have clearly been given by Christ to his church for a specific time-frame: "*until* we all attain to the unity of the faith and of the knowledge of the Son of God, to mature manhood, to the measure of the stature of the fullness of Christ" (Eph 4:13). How much clearer can Scripture be? These ascension-gifts to the church *continue* until she attains the full stature of Christ, maturity. And clearly, we are not there yet. To reject any one of these ministries is to retard the body of Christ's maturation! Ephesians 2:20 – "built on the foundation of the apostles and prophets, Christ Jesus himself being the cornerstone" – can be understood from the original to mean either the foundation which the apostles and prophets lay or themselves as constituting the foundation. Both of these suit not only the first-century apostles laying the once-for-all canonical foundation but also continuing apostles.

Present-day apostles, while constituting the foundation, must lay the once-for-all foundation of the Scriptures. Even so, the latter sense of constituting the foundation is more natural in light of 3:5 which attributes the revelation of the mystery to the then present apostles and prophets. Additionally 1 Corinthians 12:28, that "God has appointed in the church first apostles, second prophets, third teachers", indicates their foundational nature. And Ephesians 4:7-11 shows that while they have received gifts from Christ individually, they are *themselves* sent by Christ as gifts to his church corporately. The context of Ephesians 2:20 also confirms that the prophets are not OT but rather NT prophets, both first-century (3:5) and present-day (4:11-13). Furthermore, the *growing* (2:21) and *building* together (2:22) of the temple are both present active indicative, showing that "the whole structure" (v 21) – foundation *and* edifice – are in process, not a once-for-all completion. The foundation of apostles and prophets is therefore still growing as a present reality. As Ephesians

4 also shows, through *all* five ascension-gift ministries the body of Christ is still growing toward historical maturity.

Classical Pentecostals must re-evaluate, therefore, their historic, semi-cessationist rejection of apostles and prophets (e.g., the Assembly of God's official rejection in 1949). Integral to the mid-twentieth century renewal and revival movements, the foundational ministry of apostles and prophets has been the subject of re-emphasis and functional restoration, although with varying degrees of health and biblical accuracy. There is much ground to cover in this regard before the restoration is universally adopted across the body of Christ. Clearly, this demands a reformation of the church and complete recovery of apostolic ecclesiology. Our inherited pastor-centred structures continue to hinder this process, not to mention the maturity of the body and kingdom orientation. Nevertheless, there is no reason not to build prototype expressions, not only for the optimal functioning of the body of Christ now but also to prepare the way for future generations.

Tribalism and sectarianism for *apostolic unity*

Fourth, she must reject her *tribalism and sectarianism* for apostolic unity (Rom 16:16; 1 Cor 1:10; 11:18; Gal 5:20; Jude 19). This is not to deny that God sets the solitary within families (Ps 68). God has ordained that his people dwell together as families, and as tribes and as an entire holy nation. Nevertheless, where the more basic configurations degenerate into schisms and judgmentalism, dividing the house of God and the holy nation, there must be repentance and restitution. This is especially the case within local and citywide jurisdictions. This is not the place to teach it, but there is an apostolic blueprint and architecture for the spiritual and functional unity of God's people.

This is particularly pertinent for the Reformed and renewal streams of the church. As it was with the creation, so it is with the new creation. As the *Spirit of God* brooded over the waters, the heavenly hosts and the whole of history anticipated the *Word of God* powerfully calling forth *cosmos from chaos* (Gen 1).

Likewise, the renewal of the 1960s-80s, the charismatic outpouring across all denominations and nations. The Spirit of God, brooding over the chaos of the renewal, was but the harbinger of a word from God that would call forth a new order. And this word came through several globally influential renewal teachers, who were also Reformed theologically (i.e., Ern Baxter and Bob Mumford).

They brought a corrective word proclaiming the *government of God* not only over his church but also society. Carrying a burden for the unity of the church, they promoted a vision of the corporate people of God, in divine order, as a model and demonstration of his wisdom to the world. In God's providence they intersected with Rousas Rushdoony, an influential Reformed thinker and father of Christian reconstruction, and together (through publishing and conferences) seeded the renewal with a Kingdom vision and ethos, particularly for cultural reformation. As is too often the case with reformers, they were not received well by their respective movements (i.e., the renewal and Reformed movements). But as forerunners they modelled the future—the two major streams of God's activity in history flowing together to become the *mainstream*: the Word and the Spirit. And this, for one purpose: to call *cosmos out of chaos*—God's order out of the ecclesial and societal disarray of autonomous-man.

For the Reformed stream, or the renewal, to see themselves as the *mainstream* is a delusion. The *Word and the Spirit* held in balanced tension is integral to the advance of the Kingdom of God. Neither expression is complete without the other. In a day of restoration both emphases will merge as the mainstream of God's purpose in the world, releasing the full force of the Kingdom of God flowing to the healing of the nations (Ezek 47; Rev 22). In that day,

> Your watchmen shall lift up their voices,
> With their voices they shall sing together;
> For *they shall see eye to eye*
> When the LORD brings back Zion.

Isaiah 52:8 NKJV

When "the LORD brings back Zion" – the reconstruction of both church and society — the watchmen will "see eye to eye". In fact, where brothers dwell together in unity *there* the LORD "commands" a blessing— life forevermore (Ps 133). Only then will many peoples respond and say:

> "Come, let us go up to the mountain of the LORD,
>   to the house of the God of Jacob,
> that he may teach us his ways
>   and that we may walk in his paths."
> For out of Zion shall go forth the law,
>   and the word of the LORD from

Jerusalem.

Isaiah 2:3

When the inhabitants of Zion dwell together in unity God will "command" and the nations will come. Human means – marketing and advertising, promotion and programs – will be obsolete. God's Spirit will be outpoured in unusual measure and the nations will be taught of the LORD. Their political and civil leaders will come to learn of the ways and laws of God for human society.

The apostolic unity of the body of Christ demands that we not only dwell together as brothers but also strategize as co-labourers. It demands that as military allies we war with common goals and strategies. What is needed immediately is a global 20-year strategy of Christian reconstruction of church and society. This means relinquishing our sectarian independence to form alliances as one body of Christ within our regions and cities. To be not only of one mind but also to be one voice to the world.

Christ's high priestly prayer will be answered: "that they may all be one, just as you, Father, are in me, and I in you, that they also may be in us, *so that the world may believe* that you have sent me" (Jn 17:21). The spiritual and functional unity of the whole body of Christ is prophetic evangelism. The scandal of our division invites both the judgment of God and the derision of the world.

Crucially this oneness can only be found by returning to the "apostles' doctrine" (Acts 2:42)—to the historic orthodoxy of "the faith that was once for all delivered to the saints" (Jude 3). Only in this way will the church again become the ground and pillar of truth to the world.

Eschatologies of defeat for *Christ's victory in history*

Fifth, she must reject *eschatologies of defeat* for Christ's victory in history. Christ's command to his church is to occupy *until* he comes (Lk 19:13 KJV). Through his ascension to the Father and enthronement at his right hand the Kingdom *has already been inaugurated and is advancing* until fully realized in history. Christ will not come again until his church has fully occupied the nations (Acts 3:21).

According to Psalm 110 he remains seated in ascension glory until *all* his enemies have been made his footstool. Only then will he return to defeat the "*last* enemy", death, in the resurrection (1 Cor 15:25). Instead of the second coming as the hope of the church, it is rather his first coming. As the climax of the ages, it was *then* that Satan was defeated, his head crushed and sin vanquished! And it was *then*, when Jesus declared, "I saw Satan fall like lightning from heaven" (Lk 10:18). He *has been* disarmed and dispossessed! And so, his gates will not prevail against the onslaught of Christ's church (Mt 16:18). This means that in the face of seeming defeat, of insurmountable odds, the church of God will arise victorious well before the end.

History demonstrates Satan's brazen overplay of his hand. This is certainly the case in the present "culture wars", especially the WEF's *Great Reset* of 2021. The barefaced attack by the cultural and political elite in league with unelected globalists – and

weaponised by Big Money, Big Tech, and Big Pharma –
upon all things "Western" is, in fact, a demonic agenda
to unseat Christ. Western culture, once known as
"Christendom", is nothing less than a cultural
outworking of Christ's dominion in history.

The consummate example of satanic overplay,
however, is the execution of Christ in the days of his
flesh. Peter confronting the human perpetrators, delivers
a stinging indictment: "this Man, delivered over by the
predetermined plan and foreknowledge of God, you
nailed to a cross by the hands of godless men and put
Him to death" (Acts 2:23 NASB).

Diabolically animated, but nonetheless
culpable, "godless men put him to death". Nevertheless,
it was the Sovereign God's "predetermined plan" from
eternities past. Consequently, his satanic-majesty,
believing that he had sprung the consummate cosmic
coup was, instead, hung on his own gallows. The death
of Christ becoming the very death of death, so "that
through death he might destroy the one who has the
power of death, that is, the devil" (Heb 2:14). Lights out
Lucifer!

And so, the nations and their kings may
conspire against the LORD and his Anointed, to cast off
their restraints, but the LORD will have them in derision.
For he has established his King in Zion, and it is *he* who
has been given the nations – not the global elites – and
he will possess them as his inheritance and break them
with a rod of iron. Our LORD is the Governor of the
universe. Therefore the nations will be brought to book:

> Why do the nations rage
> and the peoples plot in vain?

> The kings of the earth set themselves,
>> and the rulers take counsel together,
>> against the LORD and against his
Anointed,
>> saying,
> "Let us burst their bonds apart
>> and cast away their cords from us."
>
> He who sits in the heavens laughs;
>> the Lord holds them in derision.
> Then he will speak to them in his wrath,
>> and terrify them in his fury, saying,
> "As for me, I have set my King
>> on Zion, my holy hill."
>
> I will tell of the decree:
> The LORD said to me, "You are my Son;
>> today I have begotten you.
> Ask of me, and I will make the nations your heritage,
>> and the ends of the earth your possession.
> You shall break them with a rod of iron
>> and dash them in pieces like a potter's
vessel."

Psalm 2:1–9 (cited Acts 4:25-26)

As a result every defeatist and "pessimillennial" scheme must be exorcised from the belief of the church. Or should I say *unbelief!* When Christ was enthroned at the ascension all heaven resounded with the cry that, "The kingdom of the world *has become* the kingdom of our Lord and of his Christ, and he shall reign forever and ever" (Rev 11:15).

So, *now* is the time to take sword and trowel in the right hand and the left. To wage warfare against every proud reasoning, every ideology raised up against the knowledge of God. And to rebuild the ancient ruins of Zion, the *city of God*, until she completely subsumes the *city of man*. Until a new Christian civilization emerges from the ruins of the present crisis and fills the entire earth.

This therefore demands the recovery of a biblical philosophy of history. One that sees Christ at the right hand of the Father governing "all things" for the sake of his church (Eph 1:22). That sees him as the Sovereign over history, bringing *everything* into his administration (Eph 1:10). Our vision of God, therefore, determines our view of the future and how we act – or *not* – in the present. As one well known dispensational preacher once infamously quipped, "Why polish the brass on a sinking ship!" In other words, the world is destined for destruction why bother with it. An eschatology of Christ's victory *in* history will embolden the people of God to do exploits, to confront the idols of the culture and build for the generations.

Summary conclusion

In summary we have shown that the Christian community must undergo five resets if she is to chart the way forward:

1. Partisan politics for *the politics of the Kingdom,*
2. The myth of neutrality for *a cultural gospel,*
3. Experientialism and false prophecy for *the Scriptures,*

4. Tribalism and sectarianism for *apostolic unity*, and

5. Eschatologies of defeat for *Christ's victory in history*.

Summing up, we have truncated the Gospel to personal salvation only, believing the myth of neutrality and the lie of the division of secular and sacred. We have falsely believed that our job is in the church, not in the world (especially politics), apart from perhaps some good works (welfare etc.). Because of this we have forsaken the public square. The consequent authority vacuum has precipitated a cacophony of competing voices, each new expert vying for cultural supremacy: public health experts, politicians, unelected elites, media commentators (or should I say *commissars?*), educators, mental health authorities, police and state authorities ad nauseum.

Because the church has rejected the authority of God in his word, the world has rejected it in his church. The churches, by not applying *the whole word of God to the whole of life*, have bred sentimental Christians but practical atheists. And so, the world likewise has become atheist. So goes the church, so goes the world. The salt then, having lost its savour, has been trodden under foot of men by an unbelieving culture.

In conclusion, the mandate given by our LORD is a *teaching* one (Mt 28:18-20). It calls for a recovery of the Gospel as a comprehensive world-and-life-view, reaching *from individual salvation to cultural redemption*. We must therefore embrace long-term generational change—strategies for the reconstruction of the church and society. With a biblical eschatology of

Christ and his church victorious in history, time is on our side as we labour not only for the present but for the generations.

And this demands: *first*, the urgent recovery of biblical blueprints for every sphere of society; *second*, a strategy for the re-education of church and society—because ideas have consequences our battle, first and foremost, is for minds; and *third*, the merging of Word and Spirit emphases, of Reformed and renewal streams, into the mainstream of God's Kingdom purpose to reform entire cultures and nations. Only then can *the word do the work* (1 Thes 2:13).

These five resets will prove to be God's *Great Reset!*

EXCURSUS

The Incarnation: God's Great Reset For History

> 18 Now the birth of Jesus Christ took place in this way. When his mother Mary had been betrothed to Joseph, before they came together she was found to be with child from the Holy Spirit. 19 And her husband Joseph, being a just man and unwilling to put her to shame, resolved to divorce her quietly. 20 But as he considered these things, behold, an angel of the Lord appeared to him in a dream, saying, "Joseph, son of David, do not fear to take Mary as your wife, for that which is conceived in her is from the Holy Spirit. 21 She will bear a son, and you shall call his name Jesus, for he will save his people from their sins." 22 All this took place to fulfill what the Lord had spoken by the prophet:
>
> 23 "Behold, the virgin shall conceive and bear a son,
> and they shall call his name Immanuel"
> (which means, God with us).
>
> 24 When Joseph woke from sleep, he did as the angel of the Lord commanded him: he took his wife, 25 but knew her not until she had given birth to a son. And he called his name Jesus.
>
> Matthew 1:18–25

The miracle of the incarnation – of God becoming man – is the foundation of Christianity, and, alongside the resurrection, the ground of our faith.

When the eternal *logos* (Jn 1:1) nestled into the womb of that young Hebrew girl in the form of a baby – conceived supernaturally by the Holy Spirit – an event of cosmic significance, long foreshadowed by the prophets, was coming to fruition.

For in the one who was to be born, would dwell the fullness of the Godhead bodily (Col 2:9)— truly God and yet truly man. In the one person the two natures – human and divine – would hold together unchangeably and inseparably without intermixture, the differences in no way being removed by the union. He was truly the God-man; neither the deity nor the humanity was diminished or confused. God had condescended to the human estate, taking on the form of man (yet without sin), signaling his estimation of this apex of his creation—man in his own image, created and mandated to be his vice-regent in the earth (Gen 1:26-28; Ps 8; Mt 28:18-20).

And consequently, as the *last Adam* (1 Cor 15:45), he was uniquely qualified to accomplish the divine task: to terminate and reverse the disobedience of the *first Adam* through his own obedience, and thereby, as the only mediator between God and man, not only pay the judicial penalty for sin but also perfect man (Rom 3:21-26; Heb 2:10; 5:9). He is not only the *last Adam*, terminating the old order of sin and death (Gen 3; Rom 1-3; 5:12-21), but also, and more significantly, the *second man* (1 Cor 15:47)—the beginning of a new creation (Col 1:15, 18; 2 Cor 5:17; Gal 6:15).

And so, the sweep of human history, beginning in creation and fall, finally climaxes in new creation – redemption, resurrection, and glorification – taking man and the cosmos beyond the paradisiacal state into the glorious liberty of the sons of God (Rom 8:12-30)—into the new heavens and the new earth (Isa 65:17; 66:22; 2 Pet 3:13; Rev 21:1).

The good news is that the new heavens and new earth were inaugurated in Christ. He *is* the *eschaton*—the climactic event of history. In him is signaled the 'presence of the future'—the invasion of this "present evil age" (Gal 1:4) by the powers of the "age to come" (Heb 6:5; Eph 1:21). And as Jesus taught, the Kingdom of God is like leaven that inexorably leavens the *whole* loaf (Mt 13:33); its influence invades and governs the totality of the created order. The implication of this for our eschatology is revolutionary—our Christology then, must govern our eschatology (end things).

The incarnation of Christ and the whole redemptive event signals the renovation of the cosmos—the Kingdom of God here and now in the person of the God-man – Jesus Christ – filling time-space history (Eph 1:23; 4:10). If Christ has truly vanquished sin and death (Romans) and the powers of darkness (Ephesians) in his incarnation, death, and resurrection – i.e. in real-time history, in the reigns of Caesars Augustus and Tiberius – there is no ground for defeat. This is why Jesus could announce his ultimate success in building his ecclesia and that the powers and authorities of darkness would not withstand it (Mt 16:18). Christ and his church, despite momentary setbacks, are advancing and victorious in history. The mandate to disciple whole nations and cultures in the ways of God will succeed. The dominance of Satan and his minions – human and diabolical – will be exorcised from the affairs of men— from the public square and the governance of the nations

(Gen 1:26-28; Deut 4:5-8; Ps 2; 110; Isa 2:1-4; Mt 28:18-20).

Let us celebrate the miracle of the incarnation: of God manifest in the flesh – Christ as the God-man – the champion of his people, not only to save them from their sins but to raise them up as his vice-regents in the earth, his agents of cosmic renovation. Praise the Lord!

Author Bio

David Orton has served as a pastor, teacher, and ministry leader for over 40 years. He teaches with a measure of prophetic gravitas, and as the founder of *Lifemessenger* carries a message of reformation, particularly in the Western church and culture.

He was associated for 20 years with Logos Foundation, a ministry that was not only a leader in disseminating the Charismatic renewal across the mainline denominations but also led successful campaigns in the public square, defeating the Australian Labor government's secular humanist *Bill of Rights* and national ID card, as statist incursions upon historic civil liberties.

During this time the ministry established a strategic relationship with R. J. Rushdoony, author and pioneer of the Christian Reconstruction movement, bringing him to Australia for conferences to educate the Christian public concerning the challenge of secular-humanism in the church and wider culture.

David authored the book, *Snakes in the Temple: Unmasking Idolatry in Today's Church,* issuing a call for repentance and reformation across the Western church.

David and Jenny were married in 1974 after graduating from Bible College. David holds a degree in biblical studies and Jenny in history. They are the parents of two adult children, Daniel and Virginia (both involved in the ministry), and reside on the beautiful Mornington Peninsula, Melbourne, Australia.

Lifemessenger

Our Mission
To proclaim the Gospel of God's government utilising print and electronic media, intensives, think-tanks, and conferences.

Our Scope
The scope of the message of God's government is cosmic, providing blueprints for every societal sphere.

We advocate a principle of *liberty under law*. This entails *biblical pluralism*—a plurality of institutions under God's law. Through the four covenantal spheres of the *individual*, the *familial*, the *ecclesial*, and the *civil*, government and law are not exclusively in the hands of any one institution or sphere; all other spheres – education, economic, justice etc. – arc from at least one or more of these four.

Biblical pluralism corrects any Constantinian confusion and conflation of church and state roles, obviating the tyranny of either one over the other.

Lifemessenger Inc. is a non-profit religious foundation incorporated in the state of Victoria, Australia.

PO Box 777 • Mount Eliza • VIC 3930 • Australia • www.lifemessenger.org • ABN 26 743 269 442

Subscribe today to Lifemessenger's weekly email article!

* 9 7 8 0 6 4 5 0 9 8 9 0 7 *